CW00395203

FRANCIS FRITH'S
pocket ALBUM

SHEFFIELD AND SOUTH YORKSHIRE

A POCKET ALBUM

Adapted from an original book by
CLIVE HARDY

First published in the United Kingdom in 2004 by
Frith Book Company Ltd

ISBN 1-85937-870-6

British Library Cataloguing in Publication Data

Sheffield and South Yorkshire—A Pocket Album
Adapted from an original book by Clive Hardy

Frith Book Company Ltd
Frith's Barn, Teffont,
Salisbury, Wiltshire SP3 5QP
Tel: +44 (0) 1722 716 376
Email: info@francisfrith.co.uk
www.francisfrith.co.uk

Printed and bound in Great Britain by MPG, Bodmin

Front Cover: SHEFFIELD, HIGH STREET C1960 S108110 *The colour-tinting is for
illustrative purposes only, and is not intended to be historically accurate.*

Frontispiece: Doncaster, High Street 1903 48851a

AS WITH ANY HISTORICAL DATABASE THE FRITH ARCHIVE IS CONSTANTLY
BEING CORRECTED AND IMPROVED AND THE PUBLISHERS WOULD WEL-
COME INFORMATION ON OMISSIONS OR INACCURACIES

CONTENTS

FRANCIS FRITH
VICTORIAN PIONEER

Francis Frith, founder of the world-famous photographic archive, was a complex and multi-talented man. A devout Quaker and a highly successful Victorian businessman, he was philosophic by nature and pioneering in outlook. By 1855 he had already established a wholesale grocery business in Liverpool, and sold it for the astonishing sum of £200,000, which is the equivalent today of over £15,000,000. Now in his thirties, and captivated by the new science of photography, Frith set out on a series of pioneering journeys up the Nile and to the Near East.

INTRIGUE AND EXPLORATION

He was the first photographer to venture beyond the sixth cataract of the Nile. Africa was still the mysterious 'Dark Continent', and Stanley and Livingstone's historic meeting was a decade into the future. The conditions for picture taking confound belief. He laboured for hours in his wicker dark-room in the sweltering heat of the desert, while the volatile chemicals fizzed dangerously in their trays. Back in London he exhibited his photographs and was 'rapturously cheered' by members of the Royal Society. His reputation as a photographer was made overnight.

VENTURE OF A LIFE-TIME

By the 1870s the railways had threaded their way across the country, and Bank Holidays and half-day Saturdays had been made obligatory by Act of Parliament. All of a sudden the working man and his family were able to enjoy days out, take holidays, and see a little more of the world.

With typical business acumen, Francis Frith foresaw that these new tourists would enjoy having souvenirs to commemorate their days out. For the next thirty years he travelled the country by train and by pony and trap, producing fine photographs of seaside resorts and beauty spots that were keenly bought by millions of Victorians. These prints were painstakingly pasted into family albums and pored over during the dark nights of winter, rekindling precious memories of summer excursions. Frith's studio was soon supplying retail shops all over the country, and by 1890 F Frith & Co had become the greatest specialist photographic publishing company in the world, with over 2,000 sales outlets, and pioneered the picture postcard.

FRANCIS FRITH'S LEGACY

Francis Frith had died in 1898 at his villa in Cannes, his great project still growing. The archive he created continued in business for another seventy years. By 1970 it contained over a third of a million pictures showing 7,000 British towns and villages.

Frith's legacy to us today is of immense significance and value, for the magnificent archive of evocative photographs he created provides a unique record of change in the cities, towns and villages throughout Britain over a century and more. Frith and his fellow studio photographers revisited locations many times down the years to update their views, compiling for us an enthralling and colourful pageant of British life and character.

We are fortunate that Frith was dedicated to recording the minutiae of everyday life. For it is this sheer wealth of visual data, the painstaking chronicle of changes in dress, transport, street layouts, buildings, housing, engineering and landscape that captivates us so much today, offering us a powerful link with the past and with the lives of our ancestors.

Computers have now made it possible for Frith's many thousands of images to be accessed almost instantly. The archive offers every one of us an opportunity to examine the places where we and our families have lived and worked down the years. Its images, depicting our shared past, are now bringing pleasure and enlightenment to millions around the world a century and more after his death.

SHEFFIELD AND
SOUTH YORKSHIRE
AN INTRODUCTION

IN 1974 the Local Government Act 1972 came into effect; with it a came a radical realignment of many of our county boundaries, with scant regard for history, tradition, community or identity. Southern Lancashire was butchered to create the Metropolitan Boroughs of Merseyside and Greater Manchester; Cumberland and Westmorland were abolished altogether; Rutland, England's smallest county, was dragged kicking and screaming into a merger with Leicestershire; Yorkshire, the largest county, was dissected. The provisions of the Act saw the abolition of the three Ridings, an administrative division that had served the county well for nearly a thousand years. Their place was taken by three new counties, North Yorkshire, South Yorkshire and West Yorkshire. In addition former East and West Riding territory was hived off to create something called Humberside; Lancashire and the new county of Cumbria gained parts of the western areas of the West Riding, and a part of the North Riding which included the great steel town of Middlesbrough was incorporated into the new county of Cleveland.

When South Yorkshire came into being, it was still an industrial powerhouse founded on coal, steelmaking and heavy industry centred on Sheffield, Rotherham, Doncaster and Barnsley. Twenty-five years on, things have changed. True, Sheffield is still a major steelmaking area; but it no longer provides employment on a massive scale. Coal mining paid the price for taking on the Thatcher Government in 1984. After a strike lasting just under a year, the miners were back at work with nothing to show for their stand. Retribution came in the form of closures, including profitable or potentially profitable pits; and as the remaining collieries were privatised, the NCB ceased to exist.

The earliest pictures of this area in the Frith Collection were taken in Sheffield around 1870. By this time the town's population was approaching the 240,000 mark; it would reach 284,000 in 1881, and by the beginning of the 20th century it would be over 400,000. Throughout much of the 19th century boom would follow bust for Sheffield's industries, and in 1878, though the town was experiencing the fastest population growth of any provincial town, local industry was feeling the effects of yet another slump. Brown Bailey, Midland Iron, Sheffield Forge & Rolling Mills, the Sheffield Patent Brick Co and the Yorkshire Engine Co were just a few of the firms to lay off workers and declare that they were unable to pay any dividends to their shareholders.

By the time the Frith cameraman visited Sheffield again in 1893, major changes were taking place in the town centre, possibly in connection with it being made a city. The development had begun in the 1840s when the Town Trustees began getting involved in road-widening schemes, including those at Snig Hill, Tenter Street, Trippet Lane, and Figtree Lane. In 1875 the town centre was redeveloped with the construction of Pinstone Street, Leopold Street and Surrey Street, and in 1893 the Council began a slum clearance programme in the Crofts, an area extending from the rear of the parish church to West Bar. Plans were drawn up for the erection of a new Town Hall befitting the newest city in the kingdom. Our cameraman also paid a visit to the city's parks, the Ruskin Museum which had moved to Meersbrook House a couple of years earlier, and the Mappin Art Gallery.

Frith sent a cameraman to Sheffield in 1896 to take pictures of the recently completed Town Hall, and further visits were made in 1900 and 1902. There was then a gap of nearly fifty years before photographs were taken of the city centre, the university and several parks, with a follow-up session in the mid to late 1960s. The pictures from c1955 capture something of the rebuilding and redevelopment of the city centre following the heavy damage inflicted upon it during the blitz. On one of the pictures from the 1960s we have a view of Park Hill, which when it was built was hailed by sociologists, architects and planners as being one of the country's most significant housing schemes. But then sociologists, planners and architects did not have to live in it. Even though Park Hill won the Department of Environment Design in Housing award in 1967, its residents would soon christen the place San Quentin.

The pictures of Doncaster were taken between 1895 and 1903. The site of the Roman fort of Danum, Doncaster, like Derby, had been transformed by the coming of the railways from an agricultural to an industrial town when it was chosen by the Great Northern Railway as the location for its locomotive and carriage and wagon workshops. Coal mining would also be a major employer with the nearby pits of Brodsworth, Askern Main and Hatfield Main. The early years of the 20th century saw a boom in the opening of new collieries in South Yorkshire. In 1900 the Sheepbridge Coal & Iron Co acquired an interest in the Dinnington Main Coal Co that enabled it to exploit the coalfield to the north of Kiveton Park. The first sod was cut at Brodsworth, near Doncaster, in 1905 and at Hatfield Main on 11th October 1911. The Maltby Main Colliery Co was formed in 1906 with capital of £350,000; in 1912 John Brown & Co and Sheepbridge joined forces to create the Rossington Main Colliery Co to sink a new pit at Rossington. At Hatfield it took five years to reach Barnsley bed coal, struck at a depth of 852yds. Rossington completed sinking in May 1915 and was equipped with plant capable of raising over 5000 tonnes a day.

Among the other places featured in these pages are Conisbrough, Thorne and Laughton-en-le-Morthen. This book is not an illustrated history of South Yorkshire, but simply an examination of the county through the photographs in the Frith archive. However, within these pages we hope you will find one or two interesting snippets of information. For instance: how many did they sleep to the bed in Ecclesfield workhouse? In which shop in Doncaster would middle-class housewives have killed for just to be seen doing their shopping? And why is Nicholas Sanderson of Thurlstone famous?

ENDCLIFFE WOODS 1893 / 31977

THE CANAL BASIN

1870 / S108001

The Sheffield Canal, from the basin to Tinsley, was completed in 1819. It joined the much older Don Navigation and from there went to the Stainforth & Keaby Canal, offering Sheffield manufacturers a link with the navigable River Trent and access to the ports of Hull and Grimsby. In 1905 the newly completed New Junction Canal provided a link between the Don, the Aire & Calder Navigation, and the port of Goole.

The Corporation took over the tramway system in July 1896 and lost little time converting it to electric traction. In July 1905, when the king and queen came to Sheffield to open the university, tramway takings during the visit were a staggering £6,664. In September 1906 the tramway announced record takings for the year of £70,295 and the following year the record was broken again with takings of £73,514.

FITZALAN SQUARE

1902 / 48268

Cabs await their next fares. Fares were set by the local authority: one shilling for the first mile and 6d for each additional half mile. Cabs could also be hired by the hour, the price varying on how many passengers were being carried. For 1-2 persons it was 2s, for 3-4 it was 2s 6d. Between midnight and 6am fares were charged at one and a half times the normal rate.

HIGH STREET

1900 / 45485

HIGH STREET

c1960 / S108110

In the background is the Classic Cinema, which opened as the Electra in 1911. In 1928 the Electra was one of the first cinemas in Sheffield to show part silent, part sound films. Also in the picture is one of the first Atlantean double deckers to be bought by Sheffield Transport Department, the first of which entered service in October 1959.

The High Street was one of the principal shopping areas of the city to be damaged during the air raids of December 1940. The front of the C & A store collapsed into the street following three direct hits, and around seventy people died in the Marples Hotel when it too took a direct hit and was destroyed.

HIGH STREET
C1965 / S108175

The Park Hill estate towers above Sheffield Midland station.
Hailed by architects, planners and sociologists as being one of the
country's most significant housing schemes, Park Hill won the
Department of Environment Design in Housing Award in 1967.
Vandalism was soon rife and its inhabitants preferred to call it by
another name: San Quentin.

SHEFFIELD MIDLAND STATION

c1965 / S108222

The Albany Hotel was the only temperance hotel in Sheffield to be mentioned alongside the likes of the Royal Victoria (rooms from 3s 6d, dinner 5s), the Midland, the Talbot and the Wharncliffe.

FARGATE AND SURREY STREET

1893 / 31961

FARGATE

c1955 / S108006

In the mid-1950s Sheffield was one of only a handful of cities that still had faith in its tramway system. As late as 1948 the Corporation secured a £200,000 loan from the Ministry of Transport for 35 new four-wheeled trams with all-metal bodies and fitted with air brakes, the first of which was delivered in May 1950.

The original parish church of St Peter & St Paul was built in the 12th century and rebuilt two or three hundred years later. It is famed for its Shrewsbury Chapel, which is located on the south side of the 15th-century chancel; among the monuments is one to the 6th Earl who was burdened for so many years with the task of looking after Mary, Queen of Scots.

THE PARISH CHURCH

1893 / 31963

In January 1898 the Privy Council gave its approval for Sheffield to have its own Bishopric. However, a few months later the Archbishop of York ordered the scheme abandoned on the grounds that 'it would not be desirable to proceed for some years to come'. It was not until March 1914 that Dr Hedley Burrows was invested as the first Bishop of Sheffield, being enthroned at the cathedral on 1st May.

THE CATHEDRAL

c1955 / S108035

The Sheffield branch of Thomas Cook & Son is dwarfed by its neighbour, Woodhouses. Back in 1851 Sheffield was one of the towns at the centre of a price-cutting war between the Midland and the Great Northern railway companies for the lucrative passenger traffic associated with the Great Exhibition. The GNR cut the return fare from Sheffield to just 5s; the Midland followed suit, and thanks to Thomas Cook tearing up his written agreement, the latter could reduce the fare to just two or three shillings.

FARGATE

c1955 / S108005

Designed by E Vincent Harris in the classical style featuring a Corinthian columned entrance, the City Hall was built using Darley Dale stone and completed in 1932. Inside is the Oval Hall, where up to 2,800 people can be seated for concerts. The front of the hall still bears the scars of the night during World War Two when a bomb landed to the side of the War Memorial, destroying a static water tank into the bargain.

THE CITY HALL

c1955 / S108015

In the centre of the picture is the Gaumont cinema, which opened as the Regent in 1927; to the right is Cole Brothers department store. Also featured is the Sheffield War Memorial, designed by Charles Carus Wilson and unveiled in October 1925.

BARKER'S POOL

C1965 / S108116

This view looks towards Barker's Pool, where Sheffield's first reservoir was built in 1434 to collect water from several springs on the hillside above West Bar. In the early 18th century John Goodwin and Robert Littlewood built what was really the town's first real reservoir; Barker's Pool was in fact little more than a pond. The fountain is called the Goodwin Fountain.

THE FOUNTAIN

C1965 / S108173

The gabled Renaissance-style Town Hall, built on the corner of Pinstone Street and Surrey Street, was designed by E W Mountford and completed in 1896; its official opening by Queen Victoria took place the following year. The tower is 210 ft high and topped off with a statue of Vulcan.

THE TOWN HALL

1896 / 37422

This photograph shows The Town Hall from the Peace Garden. In 1973 construction began on the Town Hall extension, a modern office block linked to the rear of the existing building by means of a first-floor bridge.

THE TOWN HALL

c1955 / S108012

NELSON HOTEL.

PUBLIC BENEFIT BOOT C°

BIRMINGHAM.   NOTTINGHAM.   BRA

THE CRIMEAN MONUMENT

1893 / 31962

The horses usually worked two- to three-hour days, whilst the crews were rostered to work up to 76 hours a week. As early as 1876 the tramway company was seeking an alternative form of traction; it even considered using traction engines to tow the cars along the streets.

TRAM TERMINUS

C1870 / S108002A

At around 7.00pm on the evening of 12 December 1940
Sheffield's air raid sirens sounded out their warning over the city.
Within a few minutes the first bombs were falling; it was Sheffield's
turn to be blitzed. Among the areas hit was the Moor, where many
shops and buildings were destroyed or badly damaged, including the
large stores belonging to Roberts Brothers and Atkinson's.

THE MOORHEAD

c1955 / S108002

Post-war reconstruction and redevelopment of the Moor was just one of many schemes to rebuild the city. As well as on commercial and retail developments, a major effort was made on housing. Between 1946-49 the Council built over three thousand new homes, as well as rebuilding others damaged during the blitz.

THE MOOR

c1960 / S108087

Pinstone Street was laid out in the mid-1870s as part of a major development of Sheffield town centre that saw wide well-planned streets replace a hotch-potch of alleyways, small workshops, stables and so on. The other streets were Surrey Street and Leopold Street.

PINSTONE STREET

c1965 / S108179

THE VICTORIA HALL

NORFOLK STREET c1955 / S108004

Sheffield Polytechnic was formed in 1969 with the amalgamation of the Sheffield Colleges of Technology and Art; the new institution was housed in purpose-built facilities on land between Howard Street and Pond Street.

THE POLYTECHNIC

c1969 / S108221

These are the original university buildings at Western Bank, built between 1903 and 1905. The university was an amalgamation of three earlier institutions, the Sheffield School of Medicine, the Firth College and the Technical School. When the university opened for business in 1905 it had just 100 full-time students.

THE UNIVERSITY

C1955 / S108049

Following the end of the Second World War, a large number of returning servicemen opted for a university education, and by 1947 Sheffield university's student population had more than doubled to 1,700. By the mid fifties it was well over 2,000. In the mid-1960s the university had embarked on an ambitious expansion programme complemented with an equally impressive building scheme. The university library is considered to be one of the finest post-Second World War buildings in the city.

THE UNIVERSITY

C1965 / S108181

Considered to be somewhat over the top for a school building, this grand edifice with its pedimented centre and end pavilions supported by Corinthian columns was designed by William Flockton and built between 1837-40 as the Wesley Proprietory Grammar School. It was later used by the King Edward VII Grammar School.

WESLEY GRAMMAR SCHOOL
1893 / 31972

St George's was one of three churches built in Sheffield between 1825 and 1830 that were originally district chapels belonging to the parish church of St Paul's. Sheffield's churches, chapels and missions ministered not only to the religious needs of the people, but were often at the very centre of community life and fulfilled many of the roles now taken up by the welfare and social services departments of local authorities.

ST GEORGE'S CHURCH

1893 / 31966

*Completed in 1789, All Saints'
survived in its original form for
less than sixty years before it was
remodelled and the west tower
added. In 1908 the east end of
the chancel was extended and the
transepts added; the gradient of
the site was such that the architect, Temple-Moore, designed a
structure supported on a round-
arched undercroft.*

ECCLESALL

THE CHURCH c1965 / S108244

In 1930 the Ecclesall Union Hospital came under local government control and was renamed Nether Edge. The institution had an interesting history. When it opened as a workhouse in 1842 there was no segregation of the poor, sick or insane. They were all housed together, and would remain so until 1865, when special wards for infectious diseases and lunatics were established in a new block.

NETHER EDGE HOSPITAL

C1955 / S108081

Around 1955 these three shops provided locals with all manner of things; meat, groceries, sweets, cigarettes, toys and hardware; there was even a lending library. Prices by the mid fifties had doubled on what they had been around 1946: a pound of sirloin cost 4s 2d, 3lb of flour 1s 3d, a dozen eggs would set you back 3s 10d and a pound of butter 2s 6d.

NETHER EDGE ROAD
AND POST OFFICE

C1955 / S108059

Nether Edge was one of the residential areas of Sheffield developed during the latter part of the Victorian era and offered a superior standard of housing to that nearer the town centre. As early as 1870, Nether Edge was linked to the town centre by the horse omnibuses owned by the Sharrow Omnibus Co, and in 1899 it was on the first route to be served by electric trams.

NETHER EDGE ROAD

c1955 / S108095

Beauchief is four miles south of Sheffield, but all that remains of the Premonstratensian Abbey founded by Robert Fitz Ranulf around 1183 is the west tower. Around 1662 a small chapel dedicated to St Thomas Beckett was built against the east wall of the tower; many of its fittings including the pulpit, Communion table and box pews date from c1664.

BEAUCHIEF

THE ABBEY c1950 / B335014

CROOKES VALLEY PARK

c1955 / S108044

Weston Park also houses the City Museum and the Mappin Art Gallery. The museum contains a collection of cutlery dating from the 16th century and the world's finest collection of Sheffield plate. As well as hosting a permanent collection of British art, the Mappin also displays loan exhibitions from the extensive collection belonging to the Graves Art Gallery.

MAPPIN ART GALLERY

1893 / 31968

EBENEZER ELLIOT'S STATUE

1893 / 31970a

Weston House and its grounds were sold by the Harrison family to the Corporation in 1873, the house itself being converted into a museum; the Mappin Art Gallery was added in 1887. The war memorial is dedicated to the officers and men of the York & Lancaster Regiment and was unveiled in 1922.

WESTON PARK MEMORIAL

C1955 / S108039

THE BOTANICAL GARDENS

1893 / 31974

Though the Gardens were opened in 1836, within four years of this picture being taken the Gardens' operating company was in financial trouble. The Town Trustees agreed to buy the Gardens for £5,445 and it was they who undertook a series of improvements.

In 1901 the lady mayoress asked the Trustees if she could use the Gardens for entertainments for children from local workhouses, orphanages and charitable institutions, to celebrate the coronation of King Edward VII. The Trustees agreed and the Gardens were closed to the public on the day.

THE BOTANICAL GARDENS

1900 / 45492

Endcliffe Woods were bought by the Council in 1885, and public access extended in 1887, when an additional nine acres were purchased through public subscription and presented to the town in celebration of Queen Victoria's Golden Jubilee. A further parcel of land was acquired in 1927.

ENDCLIFFE WOODS

1893 / 31975

In 1890 the John Ruskin Museum relocated from a house at Walkley to Meersbrook House in Meersbrook Park. The Museum housed a collection of fine art, drawings, rare books and geological specimens aimed at awakening an appreciation of art in Sheffield's skilled tradesmen. By 1953 the museum was attracting only a handful of visitors a day and the decision was taken to close it.

RUSKIN MUSEUM

1893 / 31971

Whirlow Brook House was formerly the home of Sir Walter Benton Jones. In 1946 a joint effort by the Town Trust and the J G Graves Charitable Trust secured the grounds for use as a public park. The house itself became a restaurant.

WHIRLOW BROOK PARK

c1955 / S108070

In 1899 the council took the decision to acquire the Rivelin Valley and made a number of purchases of land over the coming years. In 1921 the estate covered 245 acres, of which 194 were scheduled for a variety of uses including parkland, housing schemes, allotments and so on. Tenants of the allotments were not allowed to tend to their vegetables on Sundays.

RIVELIN VALLEY

C1955 / S108054

In September 1909 the 7623yds long Rivelin Tunnel was completed at a cost of £150,000. It took five years to build with workmen tunnelling from both ends; it carried water from the Derwent Valley to the reservoir at Rivelin.

RIVELIN DAM

C1955 / S108038

Situated five miles north of Sheffield, the large parish of Ecclesfield was semi-industrialised by the late 18th century. It even had its own workhouse, though it was not unusual for several parishes to club together and operate one between them. This particular establishment was run by a contractor who was paid a set fee per inmate. In 1797 there were 64 parishioners in the workhouse, mainly old people and children. There were 5-6 beds to each room with 2-3 persons per bed. Each bed was provided with two sheets, a blanket and a rug.

ECCLESFIELD

GENERAL VIEW 1902 / 48937

By 1821 the population of the parish was over 7,000. The
Reverend James Dixon was the vicar and Matthew Spilling the
local surgeon, while his wife Ann ran a ladies' boarding school.
Sarah Springer was in charge of the pints at the George & Dragon;
Robert Heaton was the governor of the workhouse; and Hannah
Hasland combined running a grocery shop with a drapers. The locals
were employed as nail makers, file manufacturers, flax dressers and
linen manufacturers, and Mathew Jepson was the local cooper.

ECCLESFIELD

GENERAL VIEW 1902 / 48936

WORTLEY

1904 / 53137

*It was not always quiet on the streets of Penistone; until 1910
cattle and sheep were sold in the streets on Thursdays, and many
a deal was struck over a pint or two at the Spread Eagle Hotel.
The town's original charter allowed for a weekly market to be held
every Tuesday, but for some reason it was allowed to lapse.*

PENISTONE

HIGH STREET c1960 / P154004

In 1698 the locals decided to revive Penistone's market day and applied for a new charter. However, there was strong opposition to the proposal from both Barnsley and Huddersfield. A deal was struck with Barnsley whereby they would withdraw their opposition if Penistone opted for a Thursday market.

PENISTONE

THE SPREAD EAGLE HOTEL c1960 / P154003

One famous 18th-century villager was Nicholas Sanderson. As a child Nicholas contracted smallpox which left him blind, yet he learnt to read by passing his fingers over gravestones in the churchyard. His retentive memory must have been outstanding; he learnt Latin and Greek and became a specialist at algebra. He later became professor of mathematics at Cambridge.

THURLESTONE

THE POST OFFICE c1965 / T133001

ROYSTON

THE POST OFFICE AND MIDLAND ROAD c1955 / R248001

BARNSLEY

THE TOWN CENTRE C1950 / B333002

The Town Hall dates from 1932-33, designed by Briggs & Thornley and built of Portland stone. On the left is the post office: back in 1822, when Charles Greaves was post-master, it cost a small fortune to send a letter. The rates varied according to distance; 5d to Leeds, 4d to Sheffield, 6d to Chesterfield and 11d to London.

Barnsley was founded by the monks of St John's Priory, Pontefract, after they had been granted the manor and rights to hold weekly markets and annual fairs. By the early 19th century Barnsley was a flourishing town of around 8,000 people. There were a couple of foundries and several coal mines operating, but many still earned a living working with flax or bleaching and weaving linen.

BARNSLEY

THE TOWN HALL c1948 / B333005

In 1955 home car sales passed the 500,000 mark for the first time, but most people relied on buses or trains for getting around. In an earlier age Barnsley was served by stagecoach services to and from London, Leeds, Sheffield and Doncaster. Carriers like Edward Ridsdale operated waggons throughout Yorkshire and offered a freight forwarding service to anywhere within the UK, and Pearson & Co operated a comprehensive packet service on the Barnsley Canal to places such as Hull, Wakefield, Selby, Thorne, York and Gainsboro'.

BARNSLEY

THE BUS STATION c1955 / B333037

Thorne was already a busy market town when the Stainforth &
Keadby Canal opened in 1802. The canal provided a link between
the navigable rivers Trent and Don, and with its opening Thorne
went on to enjoy a new lease of life as an inland port.

THORNE

KING STREET c1965 / T303024

At nearby Fishlake, the village church is noted for its late Norman doorway. At Thorne the church of St Nicholas has a late 13th-century tower and early 20th-century glass. The White Hart was once a posting house from which stagecoaches made daily runs to Hull, Doncaster and Sheffield.

THORNE

MARKET PLACE c1965 / T303038

St George's is considered to be one of Sir Gilbert Scott's finest designs, and was built in 1854-58 as a replacement for the original parish church which had been destroyed by fire. Despite their cumbersome looks, Humber keel boats—see the example in the foreground—carried up to fifty tonnes of cargo, were extremely manoeuvrable, could sail close to the wind, and could be handled by one man. Their origins are obscure, but their rig suggests a direct descent from the Viking trading vessels that once plied the Humber, Ouse, Don and Trent.

DONCASTER
ST GEORGE'S CHURCH
1903 / 49857

This view looks south. On the left we have Porter &
Sons, wholesale glass and china merchants, and the
imposing bulk of the Guildhall with its porticoed
entrance supported on Corinthian columns. Many of
the buildings on the right hand side of Frenchgate
were demolished in the 1960s to make way for the
Arndale Centre.

DONCASTER

FRENCHGATE 1903 / 49852

DONCASTER

BAXTERGATE 1903 / 49853

DONCASTER

ST SEPULCHRE GATE 1903 / 49850

On the left is Hodgson & Hepworth's department store. The company established a reputation for being up-market, and there was many a middle-class housewife who would have killed just to be seen doing her shopping there. The original store opened in 1875 but was destroyed by fire in January 1901. A practical sort of company, H & H had only one rule: no credit.

Had this picture been taken a few months earlier, Doncaster's then second most familiar landmark after St George's would have been captured on camera. Clock Corner, so called because of the huge clock visible the length of the street, would have been in the background on the right hand side. It was demolished in 1894.

DONCASTER

HIGH STREET 1895 / 35313

Doncaster's electric street tramway opened in 1902 and lasted until 1935, when trolley buses took over. Other tramway systems closing that year included Aberdare, Burnley, Darwen, Erith, Norwich, Preston, Warrington and the short-lived system at York.

DONCASTER

HIGH STREET 1903 / 49851

DONCASTER

STATION ROAD 1903 / 49854

By the date this picture was taken, Doncaster had been a racing centre for nearly three hundred years and had been the home of the oldest classic race, the St Leger, since its first running in 1778. The earliest grandstand was designed by John Carr of York and dates from 1776. Carr's other work includes the Crescent (1780-84) and the Great Stables (1789) at Buxton, Derbyshire, commissioned by the fifth Duke of Devonshire after seeing some of Carr's work at Wentworth Woodhouse, seat of Lord Rockingham.

DONCASTER

THE GRANDSTAND 1903 / 49856

It is said that Sprotbrough once welcomed strangers. There used to be a cross with a brass plate on it on which the following was inscribed: 'Whoso is hungry, and lists well to eat, Let him come to Sprotbrough, for his meat, And for a night and for a day, His horse shall have both corn and hay, And none shall ask him when he goes away.'

SPROTBROUGH

THE CANAL BRIDGE 1895 / 35328

*By the 1650s Lionel Copley had become one of the leading
ironmasters in South Yorkshire, thanks to a leasing arrangement
with the Earl of Shrewsbury which gave him access to
Shrewsbury charcoal woods and coal and ironstone pits. The
Copley family prospered, and Sprotbrough Hall was built by
Sir Godfrey Copley. It was demolished in 1926.*

SPROTBROUGH

THE HALL 1900 / 45304

Built out of the local creamy-white limestone, the castle keep is 90 ft high and has six semi-hexagonal buttresses which rise above it to form mini-turrets. By the mid-16th century the castle was semi-derelict: a long stretch of curtain wall had collapsed and at least one floor of the keep had fallen in. The fortress was in such poor condition that it was never garrisoned during the Civil War.

CONISBROUGH

THE CASTLE 1895 / 35318

CONISBROUGH

THE CASTLE 1895 / 35317A

Conisbrough is derived from Cyningsburgh, Anglo-Saxon for the king's fortified settlement; it features in Sir Walter Scott's novel 'Ivanhoe' as the home of Athelstan, the last of the Saxon royal line. Work on replacing the original wooden castle with one of masonry is thought to have been started by Hamelin Plantaganet, half-brother of Henry II.

Greasbrough was once described as a pleasant village 'situated on a delightful eminence'; by the early 19th century it was a farming and mining community of over 1,000. The skyline is dominated by the pinnacled tower of St Mary's Church, built in 1826 to the designs of Charles Watson and J P Pritchett. The font cover is Jacobean, and once belonged to All Saints', Rotherham.

GREASBROUGH

c1965 / G111004

This photograph was taken from All Saints' Church, itself one of the finest examples of Perpendicular architecture in Yorkshire. In the background is the Old College Hotel, a name that echoes back to the founding of the College of Jesus by the Archbishop of York in 1500. For a few brief years Rotherham became a centre of learning, until the college was closed during the Dissolution.

ROTHERHAM

TOWN CENTRE 1961 / R60042

ROTHERHAM

THE BRIDGE CHAPEL 1895 / 36241

The Chapel of Our Lady standing on Rotherham Bridge dates from the 1480s, and is one of only three such chapels in England. The original bridge was widened in 1805, though in 1924 it was restored to its original width. Both bridge and chapel are listed as ancient monuments.

Rotherham Grammar School grew out of a free school that had been endowed through royal patronage. But the days of grammar school education were numbered: the incoming Labour Government in 1964 championed the amalgamation of grammar and secondary modern schools into comprehensives, the theory being that all pupils would have a chance to succeed academically.

ROTHERHAM

THE GRAMMAR SCHOOL 1957 / R60017

Despite being an ancient settlement, Maltby was still little more than a village at the beginning of the 20th century. Then things changed. In 1902 the Sheepbridge Coal & Iron Co leased land from the Earl of Scarbrough, and in 1906 the Maltby Main Colliery Co was formed. At its height the colliery employed several thousand miners, and Maltby's population rose to over 15,000.

MALTBY

HIGH STREET C1955 / M140009

It is sale time at G T Thompson's, Maltby's local department store. Here locals could spend their money on furniture, boots and shoes, children's clothes, and ladies' and gents' outfitting. This picture could have been taken in any one of a hundred or so towns. The architectural highlight of the town as far as Pevsner was concerned was the pithead baths at Maltby Main, designed by W A Woodland and built in 1938.

MALTBY

HIGH STREET c1955 / M140005

BBC and ITV aerials proliferate above the rooftops of Maltby. Also featured is Blackham's supermarket; after all, this was in the days when there was no such thing as out-of-town retail centres, and the only connection the word 'convenience' had with shopping was in spending a penny.

MALTBY

THE CROSSROADS c1965 / M140022

WICKERSLEY

ST ALBAN'S CHURCH c1955 / W228001

A royd is a northern name for an assart, a practice going back to medieval times when the population of a hamlet cleared land, usually sufficient to make one or two fields, for crops. They would sow oats in spring which were harvested late, followed by a winter crop of rye. Royds Moor is named after a royd cleared for crops probably around the mid 12th century.

WICKERSLEY

ROYDS MOOR c1955 / W228003

Two miles south east of Rotherham, Whiston was a large village by the end of the Napoleonic Wars. By 1821 the population had passed the 850 mark; the church had both a rector (Rev Richard Lacy) and a curate (Rev Benjamin Birkitt). As well as village constable, blacksmith, and millwright, there was a collector of taxes and a collector of rates. J & W Heward ran a tannery, James White was a maltster and Richard Cutt a linen manufacturer.

WHISTON

THE POST OFFICE c1955 / W226021

Situated nine miles east of Rotherham on the A361, the village of Tickhill once had one of the most important castles in the North, built on a motte no less than 75ft high and surrounded by a wet moat 30ft wide. The original castle was built of wood, but it was replaced with stone in the early 12th century, probably by Henry I after he had confiscated the fortress from Robert de Belleme.

TICKHILL

MARKET PLACE c1955 / T136003

TICKHILL

MARKET PLACE c1955 / T136002

When this picture was taken Tickhill was in a West Riding mining area, but it had retained its rural image and appeal. As well as the castle, the parish church of St Mary's is considered to be one of the finest in Yorkshire, having been rebuilt in white magnesian limestone in the late 14th century, though some earlier parts still remain.

Founded in 1147, Roche Abbey was a colony of Newminster in Northumberland, itself a daughter of the great Cistercian abbey of Fountains. The abbey took its name from a cross-like rock that was already an object of pilgrimage for the faithful. The main ruins comprise parts of the east walls of the transepts, part of the chancel and a vaulted gatehouse.

ROCHE ABBEY

1893 / 31978

In 1538 Roche Abbey was surrendered to the Crown and destroyed.
The choir stalls were fired to melt lead; timber and stone were sold off
as the great building was reduced to little more than a quarry. Michael
Sherbrook, rector of Wickersley, wrote: 'All things of price either spoiled,
carted away, or defaced to the uttermost ... nothing was spared but the
oxhouses and swinecoates and other such houses of office, that stood
without the walls.'

ROCHE ABBEY

1893 / 31979

*Just 2¼ miles south-west of Roche Abbey stands
All Saints'. Its fine Perpendicular spire is unusual,
in that the corner walling of the belfry is sloped off.
It is also one of several churches where the architect
has employed toy flying buttresses; other examples
are St Mary's, Whittlesea and King's Sutton,
Northants.*

LAUGHTON-EN-LE-MORTHEN

ALL SAINTS' CHURCH c1965 / L526001

The independent parish of Dinnington almost cuts the parish of Laughton-en-le-Morthen in two. In the mid 11th century Dinnington was still a part of the old royal estate of Conisbrough, along with Harthill, Braithwell and Anston, though Laughton had been detached and was ruled by Earl Edwin of Mercia.

DINNINGTON

THE SQUARE c1965 / D101012

This photograph shows Lordens Hill on a somewhat gloomy day. There are few cars parked along the street, but in those days private car ownership amid working families was still something of a novelty. The average wage was around £17 a week, and the annual road fund licence was £17.10.0d. A new Ford Cortina saloon cost £669, and a Zephyr £933.

DINNINGTON

LAUGHTON ROAD c1965 / D101010

After the Norman Conquest, the lands belonging to those theyns who had either fought for Harold or were implicated in the Northern rebellions were confiscated and awarded to William's followers. One powerful Norman lord in South Yorkshire was Roger de Bully. His estates included North Anston, Greasbrough, Wickersley, Ecclesfield, Laughton-en-le-Morthen and Mexborough.

NORTH ANSTON

CROWGATE c1960 / A126018

Kiveton Park was once an estate belonging to Sir Thomas Osborne, Earl of Danby and later First Duke of Leeds; the house, designed by William Talman, has long since been demolished. In 1900 the Sheepbridge Coal & Iron Co secured an interest in the Dinnington Main Coal Co, which had been formed to exploit the coalfield to the north of Kiveton Park.

KIVETON PARK

THE METHODIST CHURCH c1965 / K81002

WALES

CHURCH STREET c1955 / W519007

At the beginning of the 11th century Wales, the 'territory of the Welshmen', was owned by the wealthy Mercian thegn Wulfric Spott, who also owned lands in Derbyshire and Staffordshire. By 1066 Spott's former lands around Wales had been divided into several manors with scattered blocks of land.

WALES

MANOR ROAD c1955 / W519003

Farm buildings in the heart of the village bear testimony to a time when most villagers worked on the land. In the days when the Reverend William Downes was rector, and William Wilkinson kept the Leeds Arms, local farmers included Joseph Booth, Jonathan Marshall, Maude Thomas, John Shirt and Thomas Stanland.

WALES

THE SQUARE c1955 / W519009

The earliest parts of All Hallows date from c1200; the chancel is 13th century, and Victorian additions include the east window and north aisle windows. Some of the stained glass is from Florence. The monuments to Lady Margaret Osborne and the First Duke of Leeds are of outstanding quality and craftsmanship.

HARTHILL

THE CHURCH c1955 / H193009

HARTHILL

WOODHALL LANE c1965 / H193019

When this picture was taken there had been a Blue Bell inn in the village for over 140 years. In the early 1820s the village had three inns. The Blue Bell was kept by F Glossop, who was also a maltster; the landlord at the White Hart was Thomas Booth; and William Clark ran the Three Crowns. The village also had a surgeon (George Frith) and a constable (George Brunt).

BASLOW

THE OLD MILL 1886 / 16576

Here we see the old bridge and the mill. A guide book for 1886 states that the village had no special feature of interest to the tourist, though its situation was pleasant and that the church with its stumpy spire was charmingly placed amid a grove of lime trees.

INDEX

PLEASE HELP US BRING FRITH'S PHOTOGRAPHS TO LIFE

Our authors do their best to recount the history of the places they write about. They give insights into how particular towns and villages developed, they describe the architecture of streets and buildings, and they discuss the lives of famous people who lived there. But however knowledgeable our authors are, the story they tell is necessarily incomplete.

Frith's photographs are so much more than plain historical documents. They are living proofs of the flow of human life down the generations. They show real people at real moments in history; and each of those people is the son or daughter of someone, the brother or sister, aunt or uncle, grandfather or grandmother of someone else. All of them lived, worked and played in the streets depicted in Frith's photographs.

We would be grateful if you would tell us about the many places shown in our photographs—the streets with their buildings, shops, businesses and industries. Describe your own memories of life in those streets: what it was like growing up there, who ran the local shop and what shopping was like years ago; if your workplace is shown tell us about your working day and what the building is used for now. With your help more and more Frith photographs can be brought to life, and vital memories preserved for posterity.

We will gradually add your comments and stories to the archive for the benefit of historians of the future. Wherever possible, we will try to include some of your comments in future editions of our books. Moreover, if you spot errors in dates, titles or other facts, please let us know, because our archive records are not always completely accurate—they rely on 150 years of human endeavour and hand-compiled records.

So please write, fax or email us with your stories and memories. Thank you!

CHOOSE ANY PHOTOGRAPH FROM THIS BOOK

for your FREE Mounted Print. Order further prints at half price

Fill in and cut out the voucher on the next page and return it with your remittance for £2.50 for postage, packing and handling to UK addresses (US $5.00 for USA and Canada). For all other overseas addresses include £5.00 post and handling.
Choose any photograph included in this book. Make sure you quote its unique reference number eg. 42365 (it is mentioned after the photograph date. 1890 / 42365). Your SEPIA print will be approx 12" x 8" and mounted in a cream mount with a burgundy rule line (overall size 14" x 11").

Mounted Print
Overall size 14 x 11 inches

Order additional Mounted Prints at HALF PRICE - If you would like to order more Frith prints from this book, possibly as gifts for friends and family, you can buy them at half price (with no extra postage and handling costs) - only £7.49 each (UK orders), US $14.99 each (USA and Canada).

---

* IMPORTANT!

These special prices are only available if you order at the same time as you order your free mounted print. You must use the ORIGINAL VOUCHER on the facing page (no copies permitted). We can only despatch to one address.

Have your Mounted Prints framed (UK orders only) - For an extra £14.95 per print you can have your mounted print(s) framed in an elegant polished wood and gilt moulding, overall size 16" x 13" (no additional postage).

FRITH PRODUCTS AND SERVICES

All Frith photographs are available for you to buy as framed or mounted prints. From time to time, other illustrated items such as Address Books, Calendars, Table Mats are also available. Already, almost 50,000 Frith archive photographs can be viewed and purchased on the internet through the Frith website.

For more detailed information on Frith companies and products, visit

www.francisfrith.co.uk

For further information, trade, or author enquiries, contact:

The Francis Frith Collection, Frith's Barn, Teffont, Salisbury SP3 5QP
Tel: +44 (0) 1722 716 376 Fax: +44 (0) 1722 716 881 Email: sales@francisfrith.co.uk

Voucher

for FREE and Reduced Price Frith Prints

Do not photocopy this voucher. Only the original is valid, so please fill it in, cut it out and return it to us with your order.

Picture ref no	Page number	Qty	Mounted @ £7.49 UK @$14.99 US	Framed + £14.95 (UK only)	US orders Total $	UK orders Total £
1		1	Free of charge* £		$	£
2			£7.49 ($14.99) £		$	£
3			£7.49 ($14.99) £		$	£
4			£7.49 ($14.99) £		$	£
5			£7.49 ($14.99) £		$	£
6			£7.49 ($14.99) £		$	£

Please allow 28 days for delivery

* Post & handling	$5.00	£2.50
Total Order Cost	US $	£

Title of this book . . . .

I enclose a cheque / postal order (UK) for £ . . . . $ . . . .
payable to 'Francis Frith Collection' (USA orders 'Frith USA Inc')

OR debit my Mastercard / Visa / Switch (UK) / Amex card / Discover (USA)
(credit cards only on non UK and US orders), card details below

Card Number

Issue No (Switch only)   Valid from (Amex/Switch)

Expires   Signature

Name Mr/Mrs/Ms . . . .

Address . . . .

. . . .

. . . .

Postcode/Zip. . . . . Country . . . .

Daytime Tel No . . . .   Valid to 31/12/06

PAYMENT CURRENCY: We only accept payment in £ Sterling or US $.
If you are ordering **from any other country, please pay by credit card**, and you will be charged in one of these currencies.